SHARK WARS

Written by John Woodward

Illustrated by Simon Mendez

Ticktock

An Hachette UK Company
www.hachette.co.uk

First published in Great Britain in 2015 by Ticktock,
an imprint of Octopus Publishing Group Ltd
Endeavour House
189 Shaftesbury Avenue
London
WC2H 8JY
www.octopusbooks.co.uk
www.ticktockbooks.co.uk

ISBN 978-1-78325-140-7
A CIP record for this book is available from the British Library.

Printed and bound in China
1 3 5 7 9 10 8 6 4 2

Author John Woodward
Commissioning Editor Anna Bowles
Designer Andy Archer
Managing Editor Karen Rigden
Art Director Miranda Snow
Production Controller Sarah Connelly
Publisher Samantha Sweeney

CONTENTS

Underwater World

Some of the deadliest predators on Earth live in the oceans. They are the big sharks – sleek, powerful hunters armed with terrifying teeth and almost supernatural hunting senses. But there are also many other amazing creatures in the sea. They may not be so **lethal**, but many are equipped with some of the most fantastic weapons in the natural world, matched by extraordinary defences.

The great white is the biggest and most feared killer shark.

Jellies and shells
*Although nearly all the biggest and most spectacular ocean animals are vertebrates, they are hugely outnumbered by the many different types of **invertebrate** – animals without backbones. These include soft-bodied creatures such as jellyfish, the spiny-skinned starfish and sea urchins, and tough-shelled crabs, lobsters and shrimps.*

When they attack their prey some sharks roll their eyes back into their heads to protect them.

Sharks constantly grow new rows of sharp teeth.

Gristle and bone
*Sharks are fish, but with skeletons made of gristly **cartilage** instead of bone. Their nearest relatives are the skates and rays, which have the same type of skeleton. There are almost 1,000 different species of these cartilaginous fish. Most fish such as tuna and herring are bony fish – a much bigger group with roughly 27,000 different species. Both types of fish are **vertebrates**, or animals with backbones.*

Saltwater crocodile
The saltwater crocodile is the world's biggest reptile, and one of the most lethal.

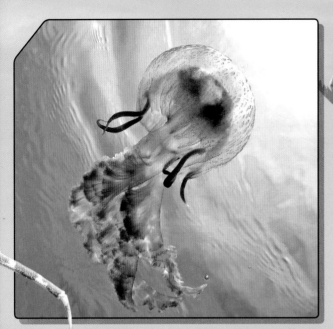

Jellyfish
*Jellyfish consist mostly of water, but may be extremely **poisonous**.*

Air breathers
Other oceanic vertebrates include reptiles such as turtles and crocodiles, and marine mammals such as whales and dolphins. These all breathe air, but are highly adapted to life in the water.

Goatfish
Bony fish like these goatfish find safety in numbers.

Creature Combat

Most of the battles in this book really happen. Many involve hunters attacking their regular prey, while others feature two killers that might run into each other and fight to the death. Sharks especially are likely to attack almost anything when maddened by the scent of blood in the water. To see how this can happen, read on...

See the deadly moray eel try to bite off more than it can chew on page 36.

Using incredible computer-generated illustrations, this book creates amazing scenes and creatures so real you'll think they're photos!

6

BATTLE FEATURES

DEADLY WEAPONS	10
SPEED AND AGILITY	10
BRUTE STRENGTH	10
BODY MASS	10
BRAIN POWER	10
TOTAL	**50**

Blue ringed octopus **venom** is 1,200 times more **toxic** than **cyanide**.

The great white is the most fearsome of all the killer sharks.

Saltwater crocodiles are strong enough to tear other creatures apart.

The sperm whale is one of the largest creatures on Earth.

Orcas are highly intelligent and hunt in organized packs.

Scoring System

Each creature's five battle features are scored out of 10, so the maximum score is 50. No single creature scores the maximum, because they all have a weak spot – or two. The creatures shown on the right are top scorers in certain categories, but check out their battles to see if those strengths really gave them the edge!

Amazing Oceans

Most marine life lives in the top 200 metres of seawater, where sunlight fuels the growth of tiny drifting **plankton**. Below the sunlit zone in deep oceans lies the twilight zone, a region of dim blue light. Below about 1000 m it's pitch black, except for the light made by living things that glow in the dark. All the animals down here eat **debris** that falls from above – or prey on each other.

The humpback anglerfish lives at depths of up to 2,000 m.

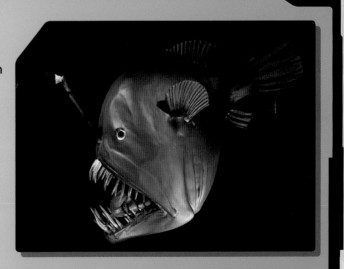

Feeding Frenzy

In the crystal water over a Caribbean reef, a school of red snapper fish glide over the coral searching for small fish to eat. But they have attracted two far more ferocious hunters. Streaking into the attack like a silver missile, a barracuda slices into a snapper with its long, fang-like teeth and chops it clean in half. At the same time a sleek blue shark appears and seizes part of the remains. Clouds of dark blood billow into the water, and its taste drives the hunters half mad. They start biting at anything that moves, including each other. As the shark feels the sting of the barracuda's teeth it whips around and slams into it, jaws gaping wide.

BLUE SHARK

0   1 m   2 m   3 m

ROLLOVER TEETH

Sharks often lose teeth when they bite into their prey. Luckily, the old teeth are always being replaced by new ones. Rows of new teeth form inside the jaws, pointing inwards. Each tooth row gradually rolls upright as older teeth move to the outside of the jaw and fall off.

Elegant and fast, the blue shark gets its name from its metallic blue back. It has a slender body and a long, pointed snout, giving it the **streamlining** it needs to cruise the oceans without tiring. Like most sharks it uses its extra-long pectoral fins like wings to give lift as it swims forward; if it stopped it would sink. It usually preys on smaller fish and squid.

BATTLE FEATURES

DEADLY WEAPONS	7
SPEED AND AGILITY	8
BRUTE STRENGTH	6
BODY MASS	6
BRAIN POWER	4
TOTAL	31

CREATURE FEATURE

Bony scales make the shark's skin very **abrasive**, like sandpaper.

Blue sharks can grow up to 3.7 m long.

Tiny, bony scales cover the body.

Old teeth fall out and new ones grow.

GREAT BARRACUDA

BATTLE FEATURES

DEADLY WEAPONS	5
SPEED AND AGILITY	6
BRUTE STRENGTH	4
BODY MASS	4
BRAIN POWER	4
TOTAL	**23**

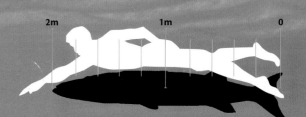

2m   1m   0

Long-bodied, silvery barracuda are among the most deadly predators of fish that live in warm seas. Young ones swim in schools, but older, bigger barracuda prowl the oceans alone, **ambushing** prey in high-speed strikes that seem to come out of nowhere. A barracuda will even attack fish as big as itself, tearing them apart with its many razor-edged teeth before gulping down each bleeding chunk.

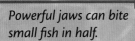

CREATURE FEATURE

A great barracuda can charge its prey at speeds of more than 40 km/h.

Streamlined body shape for speed.

Powerful jaws can bite small fish in half.

Barracudas are thin enough to twist and turn through stands of coral.

Tuna Attack

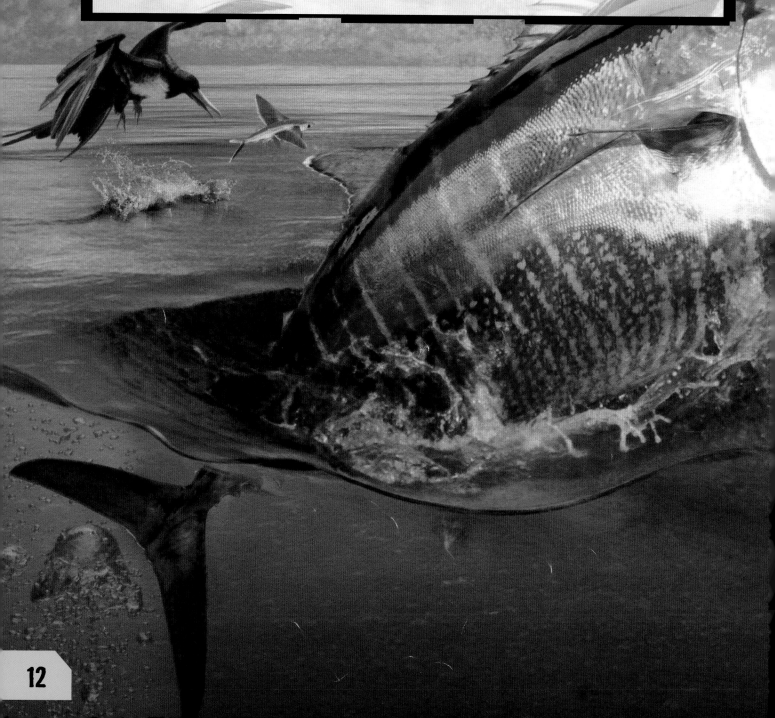

Out in the clear tropical ocean, tiny creatures drifting near the surface attract a **shoal** of hungry flying fish. Their silvery forms are hard to see against the glittering ocean surface, but this doesn't fool the tuna gliding though the darker water below. They charge the shoal at high speed. Instantly the flying fish rocket toward the surface and shoot into the air. Each unfolds two sets of wing-like fins and, propelled by a final burst of power from its tail, sails across the ocean in a long, long glide. But they are not safe yet, because a patrolling frigate bird has seen them too. Will they get away?

TUNA

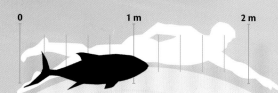

0   1 m   2 m

SUPERCHARGED

Tuna have a special blood circulation system that keeps their bodies warmer than the surrounding water, making their muscles work much more efficiently than those of most other fish. The muscles also contain a red substance that absorbs extra oxygen – the stuff that turns food into energy.

With their big, rounded bodies, tuna do not look like high-speed killers. But that is just what they are. The massive blocks of special red muscle along their flanks vibrate their tall, super-efficient tail fins to drive them through the water at blistering speed as they home in on their prey. They may even leap into the air to seize flying fish. Unlike most oceanic hunters they also hunt in shoals.

CREATURE FEATURE

Some tuna are giants, growing to 4 m long and weighing well over 600 kg.

BATTLE FEATURES

KILLER ABILITY	4
SPEED AND AGILITY	9
BRUTE STRENGTH	4
BODY MASS	6
BRAIN POWER	4
TOTAL	27

Powerful flank muscles allow tuna to swim at 70 km/h or more.

Tiny finlets help with streamlining.

Tuna can retract some of their fins to reduce drag.

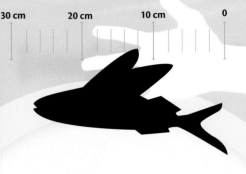

FACT FLASH

Frigatebirds soar over oceans like albatrosses, looking for animals that they can catch in flight. Flying fish make a perfect snack!

BATTLE FEATURES

KILLER ABILITY	0
SPEED AND AGILITY	8
BRUTE STRENGTH	1
BODY MASS	2
BRAIN POWER	2
TOTAL	13

CREATURE FEATURE

A four-winged flying fish can glide for 200m at speeds of almost 60 km/h.

30 cm   20 cm   10 cm   0

Flying fish are often attacked by tuna, but they are no easy target because they have an amazing escape tactic! The paired **pectoral** fins at the front of the body are much longer then usual, and as they open up they lock in place to make very efficient wings. The "four-winged" flying fish also have extended pelvic fins. Their powerful tails act like outboard motors as they streak away across the ocean surface.

Snapped mid-air, flying fish really do look like birds.

Fins close when swimming.

Big eyes work well in dim underwater light.

Winglike fins for "flying".

15

Sword Fight

In the deep blue ocean, far from land, two fish are engaged in a deadly high-speed duel. One is the fastest shark on the planet—the shortfin mako. It's in hot pursuit of its favourite prey, a swordfish. Both could outstrip almost any other fish in the sea, but the mako has the edge. Little by little it gains on its fleeing target until it is close enough to snap at its fins. The swordfish swerves, and the shark overshoots. It doubles back to renew its attack, but now they're hurtling toward each other head-on. The swordfish cannot stop, and buries its long sword deep in the mako's head. The shark is doomed, but what about the swordfish?

SWORDFISH

Streamlined like a jet fighter, right down to its very long, water-piercing bill, the swordfish is specialized for swimming faster than almost any other creature. Its super-efficient muscles and tail fin can propel it at 90 km/h or more as it chases after smaller fish and squid.

0   1 m   2 m   3 m

BATTLE FEATURES

KILLER ABILITY	5
SPEED AND AGILITY	10
BRUTE STRENGTH	6
BODY MASS	7
BRAIN POWER	4
TOTAL	**32**

CREATURE FEATURE

Swordfish have special organs that keep their brains and eyes warm.

Skin rather than scales.

No teeth. Swordfish often swallow fish whole.

Bill is used to slash at prey, but mostly for streamlining.

BATTLE FEATURES

KILLER ABILITY	8
SPEED AND AGILITY	10
BRUTE STRENGTH	7
BODY MASS	7
BRAIN POWER	6
TOTAL	38

4 m   3 m   2 m   1 m   0

CREATURE FEATURE

Mako sharks hunt mainly by sight, relying on their big, dark, cold eyes.

GUIDED MISSILES

The mako and great white shark share the same body shape – broad in the middle and pointed at each end. This gives these killers almost perfect streamlining. Just like tuna and swordfish they also propel themselves with rapid movements of their tail fins, rather than their whole bodies.

The shortfin mako is a smaller relative of the great white whark. It has the same type of body shape and tail, both highly adapted for speed. It is an open-sea hunter that patrols vast areas of ocean in search of prey, covering long distances with very little effort.

Big eyes for hunting.

Triangular teeth with razor-sharp edges.

Large gill slits.

Boxing Match

Sheltered by the coral of a tropical reef, two heavy-fisted opponents are squaring up for a fight. A mantis shrimp and a pistol shrimp are both hoping to move into a snug **crevice**, and are prepared to do battle over it. The mantis packs the biggest wallop, with a claw that can smash into an opponent at 50 mph—the fastest punch of any animal! But the pistol shrimp has a secret weapon. Holding out its oversized right claw, it snaps the moving part shut with a bang like a pistol shot. This sends a shock wave through the water that could knock its enemy dead...

MANTIS SHRIMP

0   10 cm   20 cm   30 cm

The strange-looking mantis shrimps are formidable predators that target and kill all kinds of small sea creatures. There are two types. Some have claws armed with sharp, barbed tips that they use to spear victims such as passing fish. Others have club-like claws that they use to crack the shells of their luckless prey, punching into them with such force that they are killed instantly.

BATTLE FEATURES

KILLER ABILITY	10
SPEED AND AGILITY	10
BRUTE STRENGTH	3
BODY MASS	2
BRAIN POWER	1
TOTAL	26

CREATURE FEATURE

The mantis shrimp's claw accelerates as fast as a rifle bullet.

RANGEFINDER EYES

The eyes of a mantis shrimp are on stalks. Each has a narrow band of accurate vision, like looking through a slot. Lining up its prey with one eye, the shrimp rotates the other eye so its "slot" is upright. The crossed slots converge on the target like the cross-hairs of a rifle sight. Now the shrimp is ready to strike.

Hard carapace protects against attack.

Complex eyes help target prey.

Powerful claw stuns or kills prey.

PISTOL SHRIMP

FACT FLASH

For a split second, the pistol shrimp's snapping claw generates one of the loudest sounds in the ocean – louder than most whale calls!

BATTLE FEATURES

KILLER ABILITY	10
SPEED AND AGILITY	10
BRUTE STRENGTH	2
BODY MASS	2
BRAIN POWER	1
TOTAL	25

A pistol shrimp looks very like a normal shrimp, but it has one huge, specially adapted claw. When opened, the moving part locks, cocked like the hammer of a gun. The shrimp waits until its prey is within range, then squeezes until the claw snaps shut. For a split second the report generates enough energy to stun or even kill prey. It can even crack the glass of an aquarium!

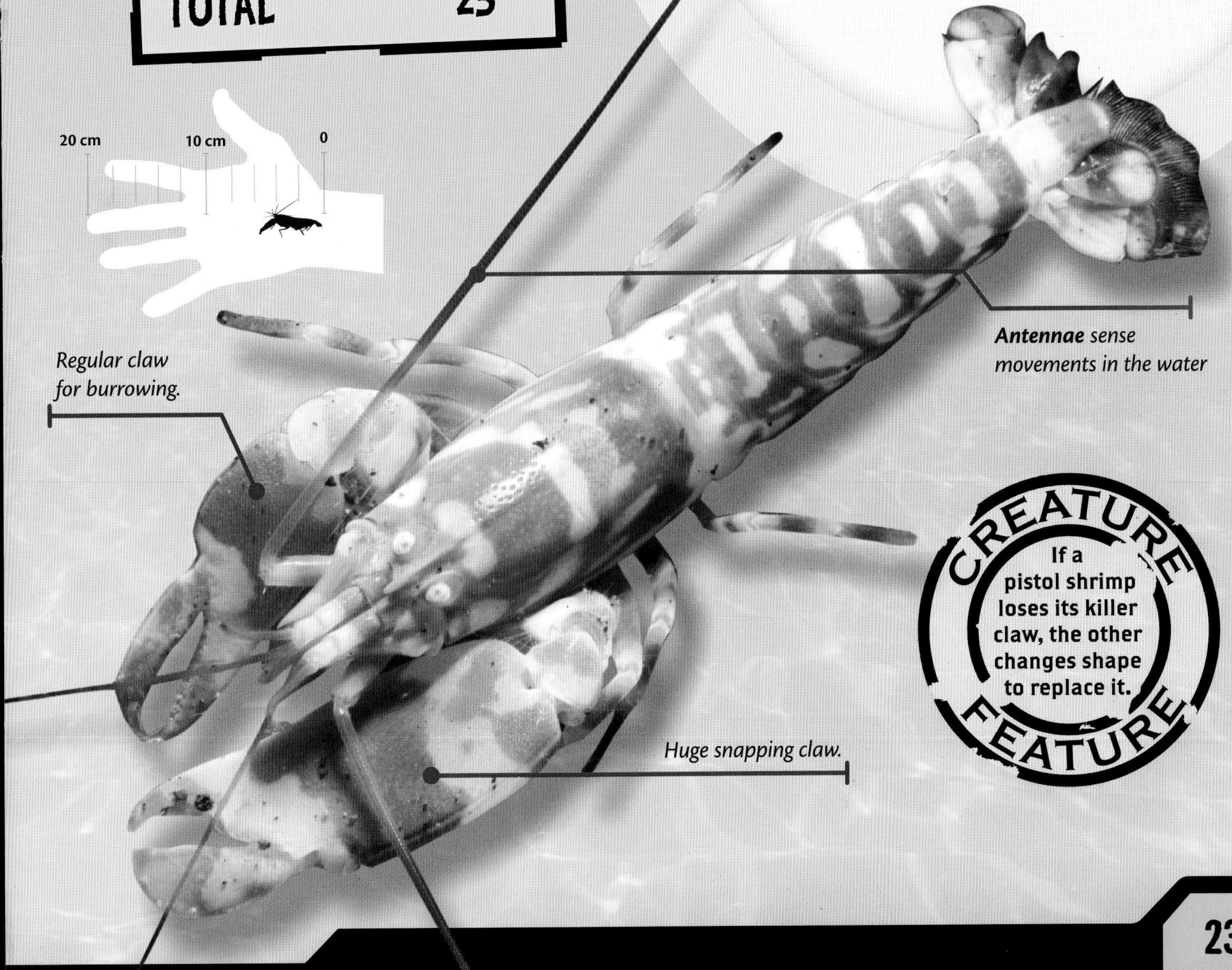

20 cm
10 cm
0
Regular claw for burrowing.
Antennae *sense movements in the water*
Huge snapping claw.

CREATURE FEATURE

If a pistol shrimp loses its killer claw, the other changes shape to replace it.

Tail Strike

In the warm Pacific off California, a shoal of **opalescent** squid hangs in the clear water, feeding on a swarm of shrimps. Out of the blue comes a thresher shark, swimming with lazy movements of its incredibly long upper tail. Seeing the squid it slips closer, then whips its tail forwards over its head at the nearest two. Dazed by the impact, they make easy prey for the shark to seize and devour. It lines up more squid, but they are wary now. As it strikes a third victim, the others turn dark red in panic. They shoot away through the water, leaving smoky clouds of ink in the sea to mask their escape and baffle their strange enemy.

THRESHER SHARK

CREATURE FEATURE

A thresher shark has more than 29 rows of small but very sharp teeth in each jaw.

A thresher shark has a hugely extended tail, with an upper **lobe** that is as long as the rest of its body. It uses this to hunt shoaling fish and squid, flicking it this way and that to herd them together, then attacking them with whipcrack blows that leave them stunned and helpless to escape its needle-sharp teeth. Thresher sharks usually hunt alone, cruising the open oceans for tasty prey.

BATTLE FEATURES

KILLER ABILITY	7
SPEED AND AGILITY	6
BRUTE STRENGTH	7
BODY MASS	7
BRAIN POWER	4
TOTAL	**31**

Muscular body capable of launching the shark out of the water (breaching).

Extended tail fin.

Big eyes for hunting in low light.

OPALESCENT SQUID

BATTLE FEATURES

KILLER ABILITY	4
SPEED AND AGILITY	6
BRUTE STRENGTH	4
BODY MASS	3
BRAIN POWER	4
TOTAL	21

Squid are relatives of octopuses, but adapted for life in the open ocean instead of the sea bed. They prey on fish and small shellfish, shooting out their long, extendable tentacles to catch them, and then seizing them in their sucker-covered arms and tearing them apart with their beak-like jaws. A squid can move very fast by jet **propulsion**, blasting water out of the muscular **mantle cavity** in its body.

LIGHT SHOW

An opalescent squid's skin is peppered with coloured cells that are revealed or hidden by muscles controlled by nerve signals. If the squid is scared, excited, or needs to hide, signals zinging through its nervous system open some cells and close others to change its colour in a split second, or make it flash different shades.

Skin full of different-coloured cells.

Big eyes for spotting danger.

CREATURE FEATURE

A squid has eight short, sucker-covered arms, and two much longer tentacles.

Long tentacles for grabbing fish.

20 cm   10 cm   0

Deepwater Killers

Deep below the sunlit ocean surface lies a dark world inhabited by nightmare hunters like the loosejaw dragonfish. Its mouth opens up to a vast trap lined with chillingly long, needle-like teeth for catching prey. But other killers are just as heavily armed, including a deep-sea anglerfish that attracts victims with a glowing **lure** suspended over its huge mouth. Seeing the eerie glow, the dragonfish cannot resist moving closer. The anglerfish can sense something nearby, but the dragonfish has detected it too. In a sudden move, one of them opens its huge mouth, seizes the other and swallows it whole. But which one?

DRAGONFISH

Prey is very scarce in the dark zone of the deep ocean, so hunters such as this dragonfish are equipped with a whole arsenal of fearsome weapons for catching anything they run into. Its jaws are enormous, bristling with teeth, and weirdly detached from its mouth so they can open up to an incredible gape. It also has an elastic stomach so it can swallow animals bigger than its own body!

CREATURE FEATURE

Despite its huge mouth the dragonfish has a small body so it doesn't need to eat much.

BATTLE FEATURES

KILLER ABILITY	8
SPEED AND AGILITY	3
BRUTE STRENGTH	3
BODY MASS	3
BRAIN POWER	3
TOTAL	**20**

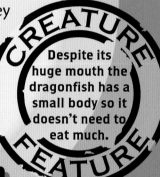

Dragonfish are seldom photographed alive. The headshot on the left is a rare live image. The dried specimen below shows off the creature's amazing hinged jaw and huge eyes.

DARK SECRET

Many deep-sea animals emit blue light that they use for signalling to each other. But the dragonfish has two red spotlights for targeting prey in the dark. It can see the red glow reflected off its victims' bodies, but since most of them are blind to red light, they have no idea they are being watched. It is as if the hunter had an infrared night-vision gunsight.

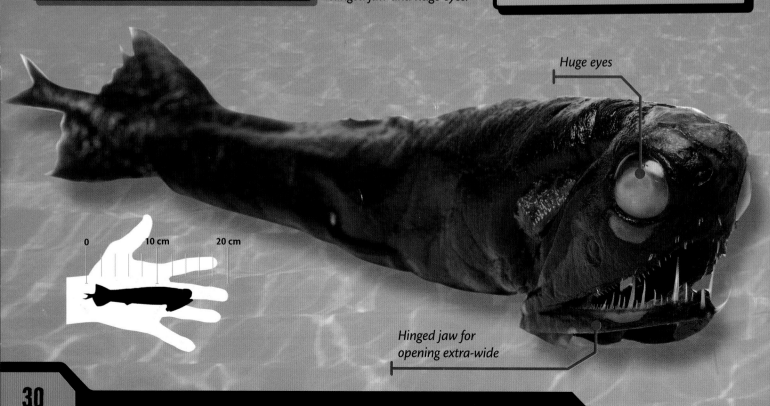

Huge eyes

Hinged jaw for opening extra-wide

0   10 cm   20 cm

DEEP-SEA ANGLERFISH

BATTLE FEATURES

KILLER ABILITY	8
SPEED AND AGILITY	3
BRUTE STRENGTH	3
BODY MASS	3
BRAIN POWER	3
TOTAL	**20**

CREATURE FEATURE

Some anglerfish are covered with long bristles that sense nearby prey.

The anglerfish are ambush killers that lure their victims to their doom by dangling an enticing bait on the end of a long "fishing rod". The lure of a deep-sea anglerfish glows with eerie blue light. Any fish that moves in close to investigate is swimming into a trap. As it brushes against the glowing lure the anglerfish gapes its cavernous mouth wide open, scoops up its victim and swallows it whole.

Bioluminescent lure.

Expandable stomach for digesting outsize meals.

Teeth that curve inwards for hooking into prey.

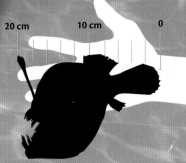

20 cm   10 cm   0

Shock Tactics

Gliding over a shallow seabed in the sunlit Mediterranean, a porbeagle shark comes across a heap of jars spilled from an ancient shipwreck. As it noses around, a flicker of movement catches its eye. It turns to find a flattened fish in the sand: a ray. It's hard to see in the dappled light, so the shark swims closer. But something is wrong. The electrical sensors that sharks use to target prey at close range detect a much stronger signal than normal. The shark backs off fast, but not fast enough. A high-voltage bolt of electricity hits it like an iron bar, knocking it senseless in the water while the ray makes its escape.

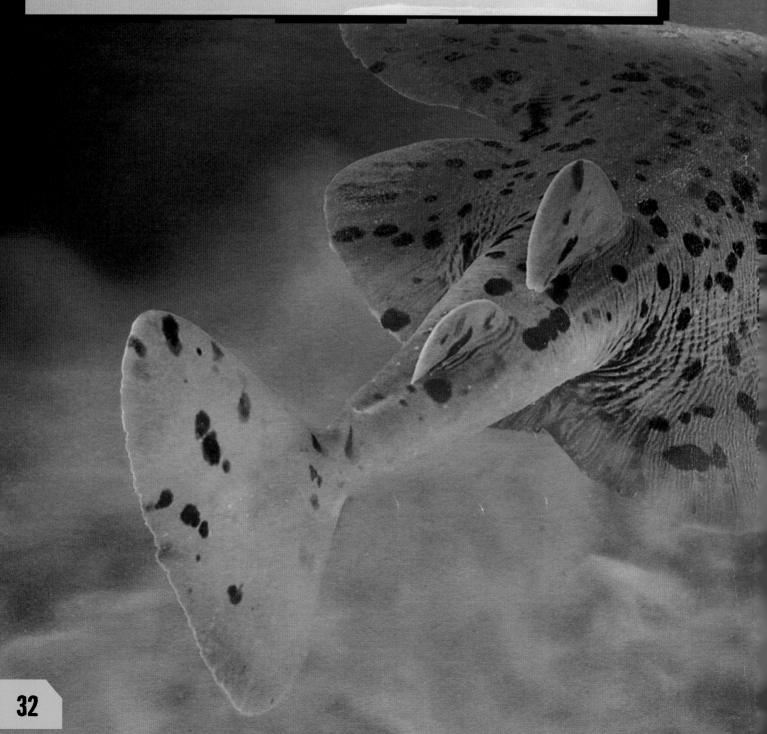

PORBEAGLE

The porbeagle is a mackerel shark – a close relative of the mako and great white sharks. Like them it is a powerful, high-speed hunter, with large eyes and long, sharp teeth. It usually targets fish and squid, and might be tempted to attack a ray on the sea bed. But tackling an electric ray is a big mistake, because its speed and teeth are useless against the ray's high-voltage defences.

BATTLE FEATURES

KILLER ABILITY	8
SPEED AND AGILITY	8
BRUTE STRENGTH	7
BODY MASS	6
BRAIN POWER	5
TOTAL	34

Stout and heavy body.

CREATURE FEATURE
The porbeagle's pointy teeth are perfectly adapted for gripping slippery fish.

Large pectoral fins

Rows of sharp teeth.

FACT FLASH

For a split second the torpedo ray can disable its enemies with a 200-volt shock, similar to the lethal shock you might get if you touched faulty electrical wiring.

3 m   2 m   1 m   0

BATTLE FEATURES

KILLER ABILITY	9
SPEED AND AGILITY	2
BRUTE STRENGTH	4
BODY MASS	4
BRAIN POWER	3
TOTAL	**22**

CREATURE FEATURE

A torpedo ray's stretchy mouth allows it to swallow its prey whole, head-first.

The lazy, bottom-living torpedo ray is a stealthy predator that creeps up on its prey and stuns or kills it with bolts of electricity. Two big electrical organs in its body each contain half a million special cells that can generate and store up to 1,000 watts of electricity. That's enough to kill small fish instantly, and leave bigger ones such as attacking sharks stunned and helpless.

Mottled skin acts as camouflage against the sea bed.

The ray's eyes are bumps on its upper surface.

The ray's gills are hidden on its underside.

Prickly Mouthful

Lurking in ambush among a tumble of rocks near a tropical seashore is a moray eel. For hours it has been waiting for prey to stray within range, and it has got lucky. Swimming slowly toward it is a fat, tasty-looking fish. The moray waits until it is very close, then darts out of its crevice to seize the fish in its needle-sharp teeth. But then the fish does something weird, inflating itself like a balloon. Short spines in its skin stick out all over its body, so the eel finds its mouth filled with a prickly ball that is getting bigger all the time. With its jaws forced as wide as they will go, the eel cannot release its grip. What will happen?

MORAY EEL

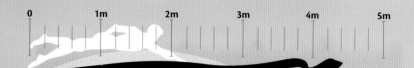

0 1m 2m 3m 4m 5m

Most moray eels are ambush predators that spend most of their time hiding in crevices among rocks and coral reefs. They have small eyes and detect prey by smell rather than sight. A moray's long teeth curve backwards, making escape almost impossible for its victims. Strangely it also has a second set of teeth in its throat that moves forward to grab prey and drag it down the eel's **gullet**.

BATTLE FEATURES

KILLER ABILITY	7
SPEED AND AGILITY	7
BRUTE STRENGTH	6
BODY MASS	5
BRAIN POWER	4
TOTAL	**29**

Sharp teeth for seizing slippery prey.

Long, slinky body that can hide in crevices.

Sticky, toxic skin.

38

PORCUPINEFISH

DEADLY REVENGE

Most predators that manage to swallow one of these regret it. Porcupinefish contain powerful poisons, and while some hunters are immune, others soon die. The poisons are also lethal to humans, but despite this the fish are eaten in Japan, where they are called fugu. Specially trained chefs remove the deadly parts, but sometimes they make mistakes!

If attacked, the porcupinefish usually tries to escape first, but if that doesn't work it inflates itself into a mouthful of spines that is almost impossible to swallow. Most hunters do not even try, and leave it alone. The porcupinefish are related to similar fish called pufferfish, which use the same defence tactic but are slightly less spiny.

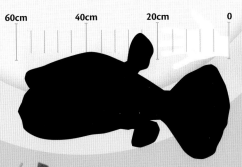

60cm   40cm   20cm   0

BATTLE FEATURES

KILLER ABILITY	9
SPEED AND AGILITY	2
BRUTE STRENGTH	2
BODY MASS	2
BRAIN POWER	2
TOTAL	17

Eyes which can swivel in all directions.

CREATURE FEATURE
The porcupinefish can look in two directions at once as its eyes move independently!

Spines that stick in a predator's throat.

Body that can expand to over double its normal size.

Baitball

Leaping and diving across the ocean at speed, a pod of dolphins locates a shoal of herring. They sense the fish by making clicking calls and listening for the echoes, but they can also turn up the volume and use much louder calls to scare the fish. This makes them bunch into a "baitball" that swirls in the water like a tornado of flashing silver. This bunching together is meant to confuse enemies, but the dolphins are not fooled. They swoop below the herring, blowing bubbles to force them into a tighter ball. Then they take turns to dart in and seize the helpless fish in their teeth, and soon the water is thick with their blood and silver scales.

DOLPHIN

Although dolphins look like sharks, they are actually small whales with sharp teeth for catching fish. They are very intelligent, hunting in groups that work together to outwit their prey. They keep in touch with a complex language of whistling calls. Other animals such as sharks and tuna listen out for these, and tag along to get a share of the action when the dolphins launch their attack.

CREATURE FEATURE

Each dolphin has its own special whistle that others use to call it up by name.

BATTLE FEATURES

KILLER ABILITY	7
SPEED AND AGILITY	8
BRUTE STRENGTH	7
BODY MASS	7
BRAIN POWER	10
TOTAL	39

Blowhole for breathing air.

Large skull holds a big, intelligent brain.

SONAR HUNTER

Like a bat chasing moths through the night sky, a dolphin targets its prey by **echolocation**. It blasts a stream of clicks out into the water, and uses the echoes reflected from fish and other objects to build a "sound-picture" in its head. This allows a dolphin to hunt with deadly accuracy in dark or cloudy water when its eyes are no use at all.

Streamlined body shape helps with speed.

HERRING SHOAL

BATTLE FEATURES

KILLER ABILITY	1
SPEED AND AGILITY	6
BRUTE STRENGTH	3
BODY MASS	3
BRAIN POWER	3
TOTAL	**16**

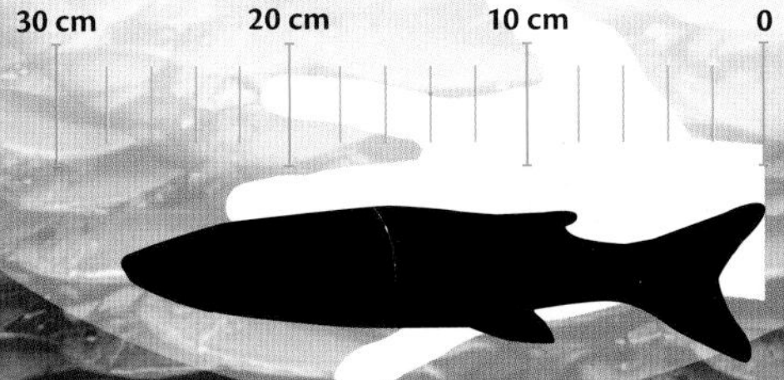

CREATURE FEATURE

The biggest herring shoals contain over a thousand million fish.

Vast shoals of herring live in northern oceans and seas, with many millions of fish swimming together in perfect formation as they feast on tiny drifting animals near the ocean surface. These shoals attract all kinds of bigger killers, from tuna and sharks to diving seabirds and huge humpback whales. A single herring on its own has no chance at all, but being part of a big shoal gives it somewhere to hide.

A vast shoal means safety in numbers.

30 cm   20 cm   10 cm   0

Pale underside makes herring hard to spot against the water surface from below.

Shiny scales dazzle predators.

Jaws!

Near a river mouth in northern Australia, a giant saltwater crocodile slips into the sea to swim to a nearby island. But lurking in the blue depths is one of the biggest, most deadly of all oceanic hunters – a great white shark. Seeing the crocodile silhouetted against the glittering surface, the shark surges up with gaping jaws. As it punches into the crocodile its jaws snap shut, driving its razor teeth into the armoured skin. But the crocodile rips free and seizes one of the shark's long fins in a grip that nothing will break. It spins in the water, trying to tear the fin away. If it succeeds, the shark is doomed, but the crocodile is losing blood fast.

GREAT WHITE SHARK

The gigantic great white is by far the largest of the killer sharks, and the most notorious. It is the only shark that regularly targets warm-blooded animals such as dolphins, seals, and even people, and it might be tempted by a crocodile. It attacks by charging straight in at high speed and using its chainsaw teeth to chop out a great chunk of flesh. If it likes the taste it comes back for more.

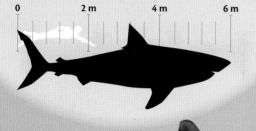

MEAT-SLICING TEETH

Most sharks have needle-like teeth for gripping slippery, struggling fish, but the triangular blades of a great white have **serrated** razor edges for slicing through tough flesh. It needs them to cut up prey such as seals, too big to swallow whole. It often rips its head sideways to saw through bone and **sinew**, shaking its victim like a terrier with a rat.

CREATURE FEATURE

Reflective eyes like a cat's help it target its prey in the underwater gloom.

BATTLE FEATURES

KILLER ABILITY	10
SPEED AND AGILITY	10
BRUTE STRENGTH	8
BODY MASS	10
BRAIN POWER	4
TOTAL	**42**

Powerful body supported by a cartilage skeleton.

Large stomach - great whites can swallow sea lions whole.

Old teeth fall out and new ones grow.

BATTLE FEATURES

KILLER ABILITY	8
SPEED AND AGILITY	6
BRUTE STRENGTH	10
BODY MASS	8
BRAIN POWER	6
TOTAL	**38**

CREATURE FEATURE

Immensely strong jaws have the most powerful bite ever recorded.

6 m   4 m   2 m   0

The biggest, of all reptiles and one of the most deadly, the saltwater crocodile is a stealth hunter that ambushes its prey in a lightning-fast attack. It targets land animals that have waded into shallow water, dragging them beneath the surface to drown. It then tears them apart by seizing limbs in its jaws and rolling over and over to rip them right off. Its acidic stomach juices digest every scrap – even the bones.

Small, deep-set eyes.

Powerful tail.

Large scales known as scutes.

Clash of the Titans

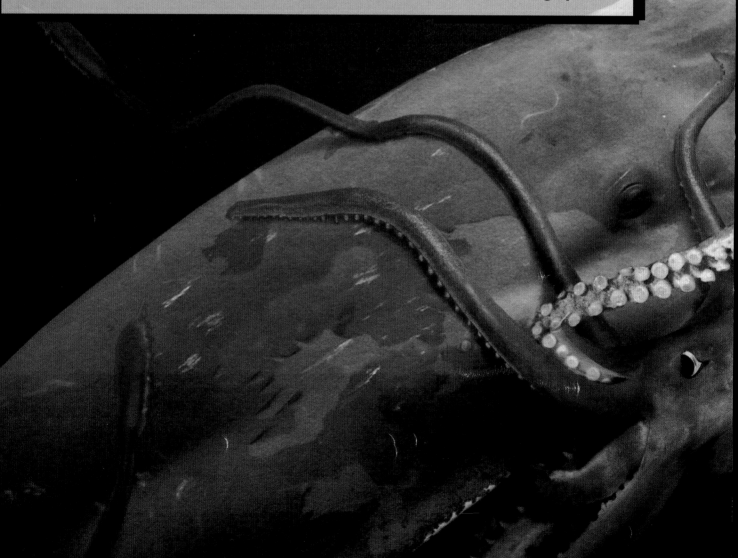

Deep below the glittering ocean surface lies the dimly lit world of the twilight zone, home of the legendary giant squid. This monster hunts other deep-sea creatures, reeling them in with a pair of extra-long tentacles armed with wickedly toothed suckers. The squid has a mortal enemy – the titanic sperm whale. Targeting it with its amazing **sonar** system, the whale seizes the squid in its teeth. But the squid fights back, wrapping its suckered arms around the whale's snout and ripping at its skin. By luck it latches onto one of the whale's eyes and tears at it. Half blinded and in pain, the whale is in trouble. But will it release its grip?

GIANT SQUID

0   5 m   10 m

Up to 5 m long from its tail tip to the ends of its arms, and with a pair of tentacles that can stretch another 8 m, the giant squid is a real-life monster of the deep. It hunts by sight, using its enormous eyes to peer into the gloom of the twilight zone and locate prey such as other squid and deepwater fish. Gripping its victims with its suckered arms, it tears them apart with its sharp beak and toothed tongue.

CREATURE FEATURE

The eyes of a giant squid are up to 27 cm across – bigger than soccer balls.

BATTLE FEATURES

KILLER ABILITY	5
SPEED AND AGILITY	8
BRUTE STRENGTH	6
BODY MASS	6
BRAIN POWER	7
TOTAL	32

Giant squid are incredibly hard to film. People have glimpsed them from deep-sea **submersibles**, but there are very few pictures of the creatures alive. Sometimes dead squid are washed ashore, then taken for study by scientists – like this above.

SPERM WHALE

DEEP DIVER

Like all whales, the sperm whale has to breathe air. But despite this it can dive more than 2 km below the ocean surface, staying underwater for over an hour! It manages this by storing oxygen in its blood and muscles. It actually breathes out before it dives, instead of breathing in. But when it surfaces it must breathe hard for ten minutes before diving again.

BATTLE FEATURES

KILLER ABILITY	7
SPEED AND AGILITY	8
BRUTE STRENGTH	10
BODY MASS	10
BRAIN POWER	8
TOTAL	43

The gigantic sperm whale is the biggest of the toothed whales, with some males up to 20 m long. It has an enormous head that accounts for a third of its length, with a gigantic boxy snout. This is filled with a substance that focuses sound waves into a beam of incredibly loud pulses, which it uses to find prey by echolocation like a dolphin. It feeds almost entirely on squid, deep in the twilight zone.

CREATURE FEATURE

The sperm whale has the largest brain of any animal on the planet.

20 m   10 m   0

Blowhole for breathing.

Enormous brain - five times the size of a human's.

FACT FLASH

The sound pulses of a hunting sperm whale are the loudest noises made by any living animal.

Huge snout which aids echolocation.

Suckers and Claws

Off the coast of Japan, two animals square up for a combat that is like a scene from another planet. One is a squirming mass of elastic, sucker-covered muscle: a giant octopus. Its opponent is another giant, but with a hard-shelled, robotic body that is all legs and claws: a giant spider crab. The octopus is a ruthless crab-killer, and it is hungry. But can it deal with a crab that has legs spanning almost 13 ft. from tip to tip? The crab backs into a rocky corner and threatens its enemy with incredibly long claws, but the octopus coils two suckered arms around them. Soon they are locked in a deadly struggle, but which will win?

GIANT OCTOPUS

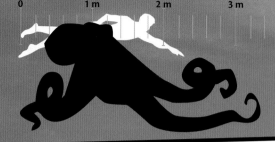

The Pacific giant octopus is the biggest of its kind, with an arm span of well over 4 m. It lives in a den among rocks on the sea bed, emerging to seize prey such as fish, meaty sea snails, and especially crabs and lobsters. Seizing them in its suckered arms, it rips them apart, cracks their shells with its horny beak, and softens their flesh with venomous saliva before scooping it out with its rasping tongue.

CREATURE FEATURE
The arms of a giant octopus are equipped with over 2,000 suckers.

ELASTIC BODY

The boneless body of an octopus allows it to **morph** itself into almost any shape it chooses. One minute it's blooming like a giant flower, the next it's shooting away through the water. It can stretch its arms like chewing gum to investigate anything that takes its interest, and squeeze its body through the smallest of gaps.

Stretchy body that can slip through gaps.

Mouth hidden in the nest of arms.

Suckers line each arm..

BATTLE FEATURES

KILLER ABILITY	8
SPEED AND AGILITY	8
BRUTE STRENGTH	8
BODY MASS	7
BRAIN POWER	8
TOTAL	**39**

GIANT SPIDER CRAB

Female spider crabs have shorter legs than the males, but they're still pretty impressive.

Looking more like some mechanical nightmare than a living creature, the giant spider crab lives on rocky sea beds off the southern shores of Japan. The jointed legs of the biggest ones could spread wide enough to clasp a car, and the males also have extremely long claws. It has a broad diet, preying on other creatures such as shellfish, and scavenging for the remains of dead fish and other scraps.

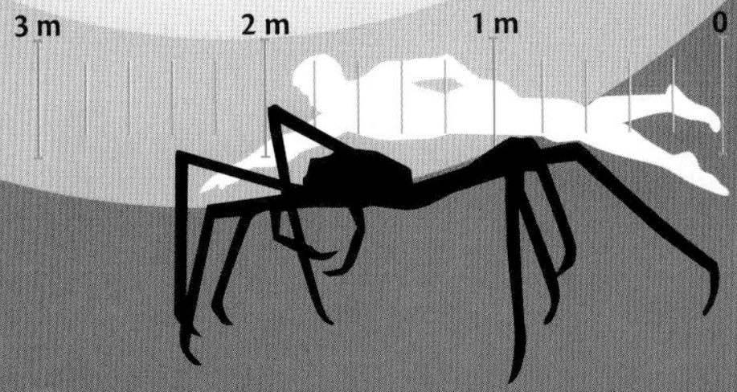

BATTLE FEATURES

KILLER ABILITY	4
SPEED AND AGILITY	4
BRUTE STRENGTH	5
BODY MASS	4
BRAIN POWER	3
TOTAL	**20**

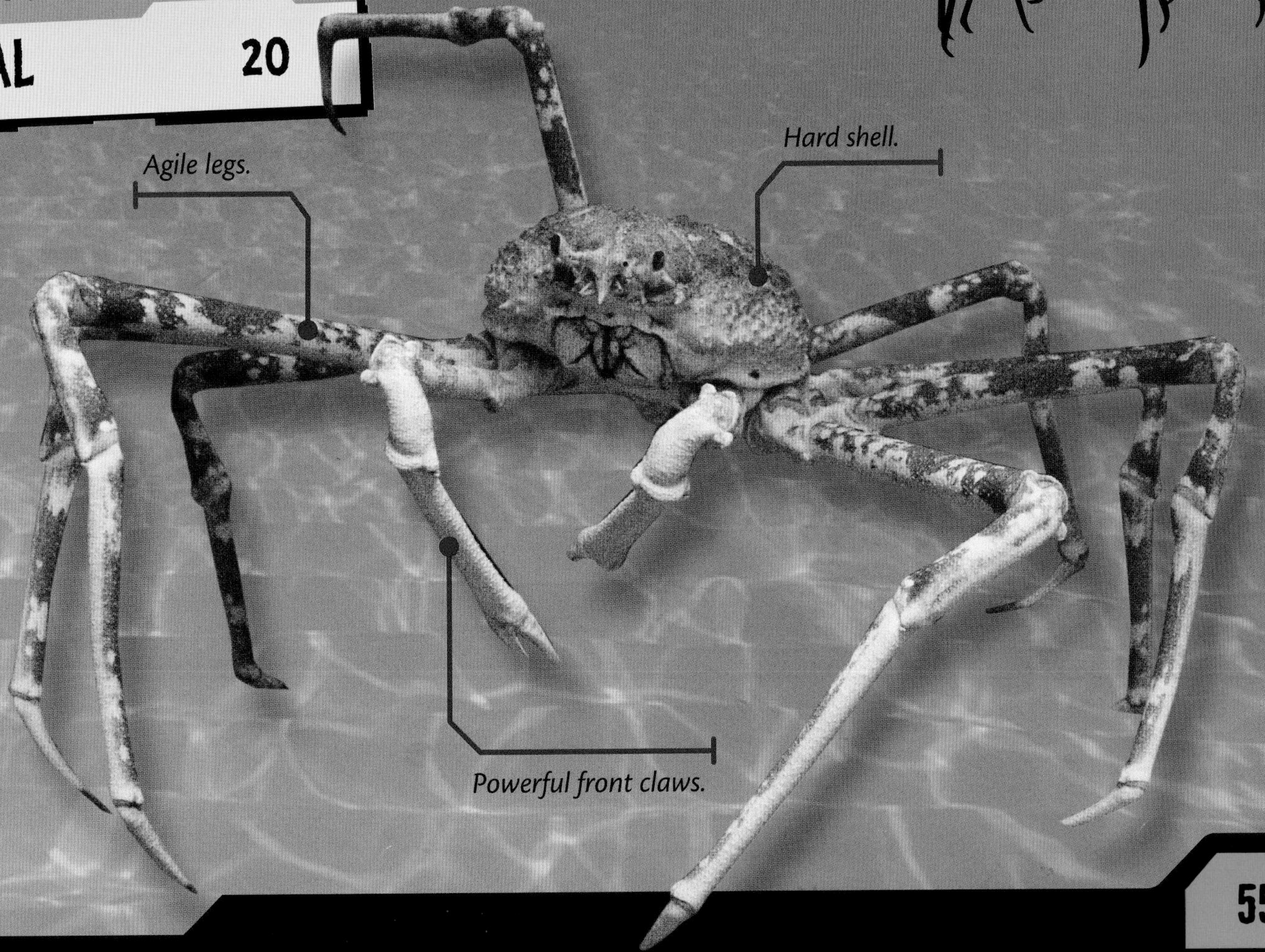

CREATURE FEATURE

The giant spider crab is the biggest **crustacean** on Earth.

3 m   2 m   1 m   0

Agile legs.

Hard shell.

Powerful front claws.

Hunting Pack

Prowling the ocean like a pack of hungry wolves, a family of four orcas – killer whales – comes across a humpback whale and her calf feeding off the icy shores of Alaska. They see a chance for a meal, if only they can distract the mother. She is much bigger than they are, but they are cunning hunters that work as a team. They chase after the pair, and as the calf tires the orcas dart between them, trying to split them up. When the mother dives, the orcas scent victory. But then she surges up from below, launches herself into the air, and crashes down on two of her enemies with lethal force. Will they survive?

ORCA

CREATURE FEATURE

The triangular dorsal fin of a male orca is twice as high as a female's.

Fiercely intelligent and massively built, the orca is the biggest of the dolphins, and one of the most powerful predators on the planet. It kills and eats sharks, seals, and other whales, as well as fish such as salmon and tuna. Each group of orcas has its own favoured prey, hunting as an organized pack to round it up and make it easier to catch. They may even make waves to tip seals off floating ice floes!

BATTLE FEATURES

KILLER ABILITY	9
SPEED AND AGILITY	8
BRUTE STRENGTH	8
BODY MASS	8
BRAIN POWER	10
TOTAL	43

0   2 m   4 m   6 m   8 m

Blubber beneath the skin keeps the whale warm.

Streamlined body shape.

Blowhole for breathing.

BUBBLE NETTING

A hunting humpback whale often forces fish into tight shoals by swimming around below them, blowing streams of bubbles. The bubbles rise around the fish like a net, driving them closer together. Then the whale lunges straight up with its mouth open, scooping up the entire shoal in one colossal mouthful.

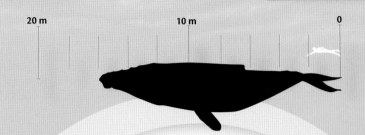

20 m   10 m   0

BATTLE FEATURES

KILLER ABILITY	5
SPEED AND AGILITY	6
BRUTE STRENGTH	10
BODY MASS	10
BRAIN POWER	9
TOTAL	40

The enormous humpback whale feeds by scooping water and prey into its vast mouth, then straining the water through a sieve-like mesh of **fibrous** plates that it has in place of teeth. It takes tiny drifting animals and small fish that live in swarms and shoals. The whales travel vast distances across the world, feeding in cold oceans in summer and then moving to warmer seas to breed.

Huge mouth for straining plankton.

Powerful tail helps with propulsion.

Throat grooves expand when the mouth opens.

CREATURE Humpbacks are famous for the way the males "sing" in the water for hours. **FEATURE**

Bloodlust

Like a dark shadow, a tiger shark glides along the steep wall of coral on the edge of a Pacific reef, following a trail of blood that might lead it to prey. But as it turns a corner it finds a great hammerhead shark, bleeding from a gash in its side. The taste of blood triggers the tiger shark's killer instinct, and it charges into the attack. Dodging aside, the hammerhead bites at one of the tiger's fins as it sweeps by. Now they are both bleeding, and both crazed by bloodlust. They slice into each other with their ripsaw teeth, but the tiger has the edge. Blood fills the water as it delivers the killing bite, and soon other dark shadows are circling...

TIGER SHARK

One of the biggest and most deadly of the killer sharks, the tiger shark hunts in warm shallow seas where it is notorious for eating anything it can swallow. Its strong hooked teeth can chop a sea turtle in half, but it also targets fish, dolphins, seabirds, and even land animals that enter the water – including human swimmers. Dead tiger sharks have even been found with oil cans and rubber tyres in their stomachs!

BATTLE FEATURES

KILLER ABILITY	10
SPEED AND AGILITY	5
BRUTE STRENGTH	8
BODY MASS	7
BRAIN POWER	4
TOTAL	34

CREATURE FEATURE
The tiger shark is named for the dark stripes on its back, which fade with age.

Keen eyes for hunting at night.

Distinctive markings are probably camouflage.

Pointed teeth with serrated edges.

GREAT HAMMERHEAD SHARK

RAY DETECTOR

The weird expanded head of a hammerhead shark is bristling with sense organs for detecting fish such as rays hiding in the sand of the sea bed. In particular, special sensors pick up the electrical signals generated by a fish's nervous system, allowing the shark to home in. All sharks can do this, but hammerheads do it best.

6 m   4 m   2 m   0

Hammerheads must be the strangest of all sharks. The great hammerhead is the biggest of them, and as with the others it has a head shaped like a wing with an eye and nostril at each tip. But it also has fearsome teeth that it uses to take huge bites out of fish to cripple them before it tears them apart. It has even been known to eat its own kind.

BATTLE FEATURES

KILLER ABILITY	8
SPEED AND AGILITY	7
BRUTE STRENGTH	7
BODY MASS	7
BRAIN POWER	4
TOTAL	33

FACT FLASH

Hammerhead sharks often eat stingrays, and seem to be immune to their poisonous spines. One was found with over 50 spines stuck in its mouth.

CREATURE FEATURE

The great hammerhead can grow to an awesome six metres long.

Eyes and nostrils located on the end of the "wing".

Wide head is used to pin prey to the seafloor.

Serrated teeth for sawing up food.

Blue for Danger

In the glittering, multi-coloured paradise of a Pacific coral reef, two killers are about to fight to the death. In the red corner is a dazzling vision of candy stripes and extra-long fin rays armed with poisonous spines – a lionfish. In the blue corner is a blue-ringed octopus, which has a venomous bite of such potency that it is one of the deadliest animals on the planet. The lionfish is defending its territory, and darts at the octopus, making it glow with warning rings of electric-blue. But the lionfish doesn't get the message. It moves in again, and in a flash the octopus has its arms around the fish's snout. If it bites, the fish is doomed.

LIONFISH

The sharp, elongated fin rays of a lionfish are laced with a venom powerful enough to kill most of the animals that might try to eat it. The fish advertises this with an eye-popping colour scheme of warning stripes, and most of the predators on its native coral reefs take the hint and leave it well alone. On its own part it preys on all sorts of small fish and other animals, seizing and swallowing them whole.

CREATURE FEATURE

Although the lionfish's venom can kill, it doesn't seem to work on sharks.

0   20cm   40 cm

BATTLE FEATURES

KILLER ABILITY	6
SPEED AND AGILITY	7
BRUTE STRENGTH	5
BODY MASS	5
BRAIN POWER	3
TOTAL	26

Venomous dorsal fin rays.

Pectoral fins are not venomous.

Bright colours warn predators the fish is poisonous.

BLUE-RINGED OCTOPUS

BATTLE FEATURES

KILLER ABILITY	10
SPEED AND AGILITY	8
BRUTE STRENGTH	4
BODY MASS	4
BRAIN POWER	8
TOTAL	**34**

Although no bigger than a man's hand, the blue-ringed octopus is more lethal than most sharks. Like all octopuses it cripples its prey with a venomous bite, but for some reason its venom is an unusually strong nerve poison, 1,200 times more toxic than cyanide! The octopus uses it to kill small crabs and prawns, as well as fish, but it will bite bigger animals to defend itself – with deadly effect.

20 cm   10 cm   0

PARALYSING VENOM

The poison of the blue-ringed octopus paralyses its prey, allowing the octopus to tear it apart and eat it. If it bites a human, the venom makes its victim's breathing muscles seize up, so he or she dies within minutes from lack of oxygen. At any one time a single small octopus carries enough venom to kill 26 adults, or twice as many children.

Flexible body can squeeze into crevices.

CREATURE FEATURE

The octopus bites with a horny beak that is like the beak of a bird.

Suckers cover the underside of every tentacle.

Blue rings throb when the octopus is agitated.

Trail of Death

With a graceful pulsing of its soft bell-shaped body, a big lion's mane jellyfish pushes slowly through the cool green north Atlantic. It trails hundreds of sticky tentacles, each armed with thousands of stinging cells that cause searing pain to anyone who touches them, and can even kill. Any animals such as fish that are ensnared in them are instantly **paralysed**, then reeled in and devoured. The jellyfish is feasting on one of its victims when a giant leatherback turtle sweeps into view, propelled by powerful strokes of its long front flippers. Leatherbacks eat jellyfish, but will it dare attack an animal with such murderous stinging power?

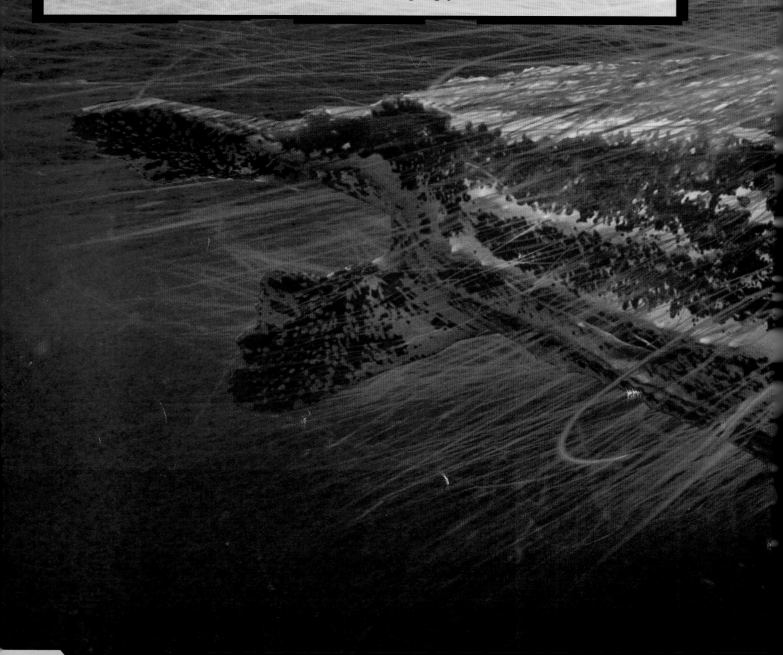

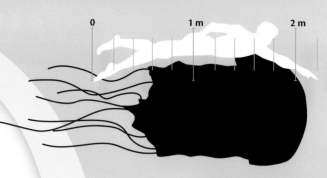

LION'S MANE

T he biggest of all jellyfish, the lion's mane owes its name to the way its luxuriant mass of orange tentacles looks like the tawny mane of a male lion. Its body can grow to well over 2 m across, and the longest of its stinging tentacles can trail behind it for over 30 m – the length of a blue whale! Like all jellyfish it is a very simple animal, with no proper brain, but that doesn't stop it being extremely dangerous.

CREATURE FEATURE

It is likely that the lion's mane lives longer than any animal on the planet.

BATTLE FEATURES

KILLER ABILITY	7
SPEED AND AGILITY	2
BRUTE STRENGTH	2
BODY MASS	5
BRAIN POWER	0
TOTAL	**16**

Bell can be up to 2 m wide.

Body made of 95 per cent water.

STINGING CELLS

The tentacles of the lion's mane jellyfish are peppered with tiny stinging cells called **nematocysts**. Each of these cells contains a **microscopic** spring-loaded harpoon with a venomous tip, packed in a capsule with a hair-trigger lid. If another creature brushes against the lid it flips open and the harpoon fires, injecting a dose of paralysing venom.

Venomous trailing tentacles.

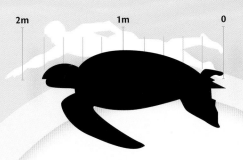

LEATHERBACK TURTLE

BATTLE FEATURES

KILLER ABILITY	5
SPEED AND AGILITY	8
BRUTE STRENGTH	6
BODY MASS	7
BRAIN POWER	4
TOTAL	**30**

2m   1m   0

Like the lion's mane, the leatherback turtle is a record-breaking giant. The biggest ever found was a colossal 3 m long from head to tail. It is specialized for eating jellyfish, its gullet lined with fleshy, downward-pointing spikes to ensure every slippery mouthful ends up in its stomach. It is clearly not put off by the stinging cells of its prey, but the lion's mane jellyfish has a lot more of them than most.

Mouth contains dozens of sharp teeth.

Leathery shell for protection.

Huge front flippers for swimming.

FACT FLASH

Many leatherback turtles are dying because they swallow drifting plastic bags, mistaking them for jellyfish. The bags choke and poison them.

CREATURE FEATURE

A leatherback can swim at an amazing 35 km/h – faster than most sharks.

Starfish Plague

On the fringes of a coral reef in the Red Sea, the coral is under attack. A swarm of spiny crown-of-thorns starfish has overrun the reef, devouring the living corals and leaving a trail of death and destruction. Protected by their sharp, venomous spines, they are almost immune to attack themselves. But one animal is ready to take them on – a spectacularly big sea snail called the giant triton. Gliding over the coral like a knight in armour, it seizes the nearest starfish and clamps it to the reef with its muscular foot. It slices through the spiny skin with its saw-toothed tongue and, pushing its long snout inside, eats the starfish alive.

CROWN-OF-THORNS

0   20 cm   40 cm

At over 30 cm across, the crown-of-thorns starfish is a monster of its kind, with up to 21 arms bristling with long, sharp, venom-soaked spines. It feeds on living coral by turning its stomach inside-out through its central mouth to smother its prey and drench it with toxic digestive juices. They turn the coral's tissues to soup, which the starfish slowly sucks up. All that is left is the coral's stony skeleton.

CREATURE FEATURE
The poisoned spines of the crown-of-thorns can give people very painful stings.

BATTLE FEATURES

KILLER ABILITY	5
SPEED AND AGILITY	1
BRUTE STRENGTH	2
BODY MASS	3
BRAIN POWER	1
TOTAL	12

Flexible arms

STARFISH PLAGUES

Crown-of-thorns starfish usually feed alone or in isolated groups. But they can multiply into voracious armies of thousands or even millions, which overrun entire reefs and may kill up to 90 per cent of the corals. These starfish plagues can be very destructive, but if the reef is healthy in other ways the corals eventually recover and start growing again.

Venomous spines.

Reef coral is prey.

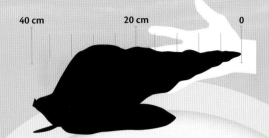

40 cm   20 cm   0

BATTLE FEATURES

KILLER ABILITY	6
SPEED AND AGILITY	2
BRUTE STRENGTH	3
BODY MASS	2
BRAIN POWER	2
TOTAL	15

The giant triton is a big marine **mollusc**. It has a body just like that of a garden snail, but it is armed with a sharp, rasping tongue that is specially adapted for attacking spiny-skinned starfish. It is famous for its beautiful spiral shell, but hunting by shell-collectors has made it rare on some reefs. This may be one reason why the coral-devouring crown-of-thorns starfish swarms seem to be getting bigger.

Hard shell for protection.

CREATURE FEATURE

The spiral shell of the giant triton can grow to at least 40 cm long.

Antennae like a snail's.

Soft foot for crawling across the sea bed.

Which of these sea creatures won the day? Were they always the ones with the biggest, sharpest teeth?

BLUE SHARK VS BARRACUDA

FEEDING FRENZY
Despite its own sharp teeth the barracuda stands no chance against the killer jaws of the blue shark.

TUNA VS FLYING FISH

TUNA ATTACK
The tuna seize a few flying fish and the frigatebird picks off a couple more, but most make a clean getaway.

SWORDFISH VS MAKO SHARK

SWORD FIGHT
As the shark writhes in agony it snaps off the swordfish's bill, so it is likely that neither will survive.

MANTIS SHRIMP VS PISTOL SHRIMP

BOXING MATCH
If the mantis shrimp lands its punch, it will kill its opponent. But the pistol shrimp might strike first...

THRESHER SHARK VS OPALESCENT SQUID

TAIL STRIKE
The shark snaps up three squid, but the others are far too quick for it, despite its whiplash tail.

DRAGONFISH VS ANGLERFISH

DEEPWATER KILLERS
The anglerfish takes the dragonfish by surprise and snaps it up. It never really stood a chance.

PORBEAGLE VS TORPEDO RAY

SHOCK TACTICS
This looks bad for the porbeagle. If it doesn't keep moving to drive water through its gills, it will surely die.

MORAY EEL VS PORCUPINEFISH

PRICKLY MOUTHFUL
With its teeth wedged in the porcupinefish, the eel will choke and die, but the fish will never be able to escape its grip.

DOLPHINS VS HERRING

BAITBALL
Hundreds of fish die in the dolphin attack, but thousands more escape. The dolphins can't eat them all!

GREAT WHITE SHARK VS SALTWATER CROCODILE

JAWS!
As blood pours from its lacerated belly the crocodile loses its grip, allowing the shark to tear it apart.

GIANT SQUID VS SPERM WHALE

CLASH OF THE TITANS
The squid will never escape alive, but its toothed suckers will leave deep scars in the whale's skin.

GIANT OCTOPUS VS GIANT SPIDER CRAB

SUCKERS AND CLAWS
Much stronger than the crab, the octopus will soon overpower it and pull it apart for its supper.

ORCAS VS HUMPBACK WHALES

HUNTING PACK
With one orca injured by the mother whale's counter-attack the hunters back off. But they might be back...

TIGER SHARK VS HAMMERHEAD SHARK

BLOODLUST
Although the tiger shark wins this battle, its wounds attract other sharks that will probably kill and eat it.

LIONFISH VS BLUE-RINGED OCTOPUS

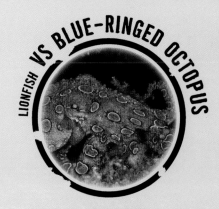

BLUE FOR DANGER
The octopus would rather not waste its venom, but has no choice. Within seconds the fish is stone dead.

LION'S MANE VS LEATHERBACK TURTLE

TRAIL OF DEATH
The turtle takes no notice of the jellyfish's stings, seizes it in its jaws, and squeezes it down its throat.

CROWN-OF-THORNS VS GIANT TRITON

STARFISH PLAGUE
The triton devours one or two starfish, but there are far more than it can eat, so the reef is still in trouble.

Glossary

abrasive
Rough or painful to the touch, like sandpaper.

ambush
A surprise attack by someone or something lying in wait in a hidden place.

antenna (plural antennae)
Long, slim, bendy feelers on the head, seen on shrimps, snails and the giant triton.

bioluminescence
The light given off by some deep-sea fish, created by tiny glowing bacteria living in their bodies.

cartilage
Firm and bendy bodily material, not as strong as bone.

cavity
An empty hole within something solid.

cell
The smallest unit of the material that makes up living bodies.

crevice
A narrow opening or crack, usually in a rock or a wall.

crustaceans
Creatures with jointed legs that mostly live in water, such as crabs, lobsters, shrimps, prawns and krill.

cyanide
A salt made from a very toxic acid, sometimes used to poison people.

debris
Scattered, leftover pieces of rubbish and parts of bodies.

echolocation
A system that whales and dolphins use to find things by sending out sound waves which reflect off the objects.

fibrous
Made of fibres, which are like threads.

gristle
Tough, chewy cartilage.

gullet
The passage that food goes through to get from the mouth to the stomach.

invertebrate
An animal without a backbone, such as jellyfish, molluscs and sharks.

lethal
Harmful and strong enough to kill.

lobe
A slightly round and flat part of the body which hangs from another part.

lure
A body part used to attract other creatures, like the anglerfish's hanging light.

mantle
A covering.

microscopic
So small that it can only be seen with a microscope.

mollusc
An invertebrate with a soft body and usually also a shell, living in water or damp conditions, like a snail, mussel and octopus.

morph
Change smoothly from one thing to another.

mucus
A slimy substance that doesn't come off in water, sometimes given off by animals to make them slippery or in order to protect themselves.

nematocyst
A special kind of cell containing a venomous thread that can be shot out for self-defence or catching prey.

opalescent
Having lots of small points of colour moving against a pale or dark background.

paralyse
To partly or completely stop something from being able to move.

pectoral
Found on the breast or chest.

plankton
Very tiny organisms that float in the sea or fresh water, eaten by whales and smaller fish.

poison
A substance capable of causing illness or death.

propulsion
The movement of being driven or pushed forwards.

serrated
Something that has a jagged edge.

shoal
A large group of fish swimming together.

sinew
A piece of tough bodily material that holds muscle and bone together.

sonar
A system that finds objects underwater by echolocation.

streamlining
Making something smoother and less resistant to air or water or moving past it, in order to increase its speed of movement.

submersible
A small boat designed to work when underwater.

toxic
Harmful and poisonous.

venom
A substance given off by animals such as a lionfish, jellyfish and octopus, which causes pain, paralysis or even death when jabbed in, as by spines or tentacles.

vertebrate
An animal with a backbone, such as tuna and herring fish, turtles, crocodiles, whales and dolphins.

Picture Credits